Before It All Vanishes

poems by

Lois Levinson

Finishing Line Press
Georgetown, Kentucky

Before It All Vanishes

ACKNOWLEDGMENTS

I thank the editors of Finishing Line Press for publishing my chapbook, *Crane Dance*, which contains some of the poems appearing in this volume.

My gratitude to the editors of these journals for publishing the following poems:
Bird's Thumb: "Migrations", "Ephemeral Pond" and "In the Night"
Clementine Poetry Journal: "Flocked"
The Corner Club Press: "At the Consignment Shop"
These Fragile Lilacs: "My Grandmother's Secretary"
Mountain Gazette: "That House on Berry Avenue"
The Literary Nest: "Poet in Fog"
Gravel: "A Sidelong Look"
Literary Mama: "Catching the School Bus"
Mount Hope: "Murmuration", "Bird at Work" and "West of Ramona"
Yew Journal: "November Nests" and "On a Ragged Point"

My heartfelt thanks to John Brehm for his expert guidance, generosity and encouragement. Thanks also to Chris Ransick and Elizabeth Robinson, my teachers and mentors in the Poetry Book Project at Lighthouse Writers Workshop. My love and gratitude to my cohort in the Poetry Book Project: Connie Zumpf, Kirsten Morgan, Gail ben Ezra, Diane Alters and Erika Walker, and to Harriet Stratton for their constant support and sound advice and for all I've learned from their poetry. And a special thank you to my husband, Mark, and my son, Daniel, for their love and pride in my work.

Publisher: Leah Maines
Editor: Christen Kincaid
Cover Art: Daniel A. Levinson
Author Photo: Mark Levinson
Cover Design: Daniel A. Levinson

Printed in the USA on acid-free paper.
Order online: www.finishinglinepress.com
also available on amazon.com

Author inquiries and mail orders:
Finishing Line Press
P. O. Box 1626
Georgetown, Kentucky 40324
U. S. A.

Table of Contents

I. This Place You Thought You Knew

II. Off the Map

III. A Brief Passage

For Mark and Daniel

I. This Place You Thought You Knew

Poet in Fog

Morning on a mountain trail,
trees shed their sharp outlines,
and the sky turns to silver.
Luminous veils swathe branches
as fog engulfs the forest,
and a shade of translucent pearls
descends around you.
Mist obscures distance, blurs
what is close at hand,
upsets your perception
of near, far, up and down.
This place you thought
you knew looms larger,
space stretched,
shapes twisted.
Droplets jewel spider webs,
give them heft, solidity,
while spruce and fir seem
insubstantial as gossamer.
Colors dissolve. Your ears
feel full of fluff, muffle sounds.
You inhale sodden air,
breathe in a piece of the sky,
open your mouth and taste
droplets on your tongue.
A poem swirls about you
like a long silky skirt
as you dance inside a cloud.
Alone in this vaporous landscape,
you are untethered, free
of the obligations of gravity.

Out of Focus

Myopic,
astigmatic
optometrist's daughter,
I was that awkward
seven-year-old in glasses,
overcorrected lenses
that made images shriek
like a squeaky violin.

Clarity has its advantages,
but I prefer
the ambiguities
of nearsightedness.

When I take off my glasses
hard edges dissolve,
boundaries blur,
colors merge,
solids undulate,
ordinary objects
appear extraordinary.

Vision, like memory,
a beam of light that
bends in all directions.

Images emerge
in the mist
and perch—
songbirds
on the branches
of a poem.

Ephemeral Pond

A poem is taking shape in my brain
like an ephemeral pond after a storm,
an entire ecosystem that unfolds
in a place I thought was dry land.

Only yesterday I made my way through
withered grasses, suffered those desiccated
seeds with prickly edges that stick
to your shoes and poke through your socks.

Today in that very spot a pond emerges:
blue-winged teal and mallards dabble
in its waters, and snowy egrets
on black stilts step high at its shoreline.

Now a great blue heron glides in
to the water's edge, folds its impressive
wingspan and waits for the fish.
Can there be fish in an ephemeral pond?

Marsh grasses and reeds sprout up,
and frogs croak in the cattails.
Above the playa, dragonflies take flight,
and violet green swallows swoop and dive

for insects on the wing. Red-winged blackbirds
perch on reeds and croon their *po-poreeee*.
Unseen in the greenery, a tiny common
yellowthroat belts out his *witchety, witchety* aria.

I throw off my shoes and socks,
plunge my feet into the nascent water,
inhale its earthy scent, reach in to pluck
waterborne leaves and feel their slimy skins.

I must write the poem before it all vanishes.

At the Consignment Shop

Ornate dinner plates once enshrined
on the altars of china cabinets
now sit on the shop shelf,
abandoned dogs in a shelter.
Translucent Lenox teacups nestle
in their delicate saucers,
elderly ladies with coiffed
white hair and diaphanous skin.
A mishmash of Wedgwood
serving dishes have massed
together on a table, deep blue
refugees from different sets.
In the window, Waterford crystal
goblets rise up on their long necks,
round mouths imploring me
to take them home and fill them.

It is a mausoleum of wedding china,
nameless marble-colored monuments,
stacks of fragile dishes treated with
such care they outlasted their owners,
inherited by children with ambivalent
memories of those family dinners
when our mothers used the good china.
Today I haul in boxes of my mother's
antique fish plates and deposit them
with the other relics discarded
by unsentimental sons and daughters,
anxious to be unburdened
of the breakable icons of their childhood.

My Grandmother's Secretary

Had she been born a century later,
my grandmother might have taken charge
of a corporation or a college,
maybe even a small country.

But in her day, a strong smart woman
stayed home and spent the full force
of her personality on her family,
or so my mother told me.

The secretary was the fortress
from which my grandmother ruled,
a formidable mahogany desk, replete
with pigeonholes and secret drawers.

She occupies it still.
Each time I open its glass cabinet doors,
a sound escapes with the timbre of her voice,
and just a hint of a New York accent.

When I raise the slant-top cover, I see her,
crocheted shawl around her shoulders,
fountain pen in hand, writing letters
in her lacy script to her dwindling retinue.

Near the end of her life, she retreated
to the secretary, crumpling, hiding,
sometimes destroying her treasures,
as though the enemy were at the gates.

She left layers of artifacts in its recesses:
a photo of my grandfather as a young man,
a browned clipping of a brother's obituary,
a single marcasite earring wrapped in a tissue.

Each time I sit down to write
I have to nudge her aside.

Friday Mornings at the Beauty Parlor

Every Friday morning my mother had her hair
shampooed and set at the beauty parlor.
Her hairdresser would wind her thick straight hair
tightly around the wire rollers, coat the job

with a generous hosing of something fragrant and sticky,
then place her in a seat under the hooded dryers
with the other Friday ladies-in-rollers,
adjust the heat and leave her to gently cook.

Once dry and the rollers removed, her hair would be
brushed and teased into a voluminous snarl
and doused with a toxic coating of hairspray
until it achieved the texture and density

of wire mesh, then tortured and lacquered
into a helmet–like structure that felt like nothing living,
but that framed her face in a way that always made
my father smile and tell her she was beautiful.

The hairdo had to last all week, so she slept
in a hairnet to keep it intact, wore a plastic rain bonnet
to protect it from weather, and managed to keep
the poor tangled creature alive until the following Friday

when the ladies would again gather under the dryers,
sharing stories of face lifts, miscarriages,
infidelities, business failures, cancers, divorces,
ungrateful children, and celebrity scandals.

But the hairdresser's litany of disastrous relationships,
narrated in mesmerizing detail as she fixed their hair,
was soap opera enough to sustain them for the week
and to keep them coming back.

Her final hairdresser, Julie, would pick up my mother
at her apartment, wheelchair and all,
and drive her to the beauty parlor on Friday mornings.
At my mother's funeral, she sat in front and wept.

Ancient

Bristlecone pine
high on the
mountain, your
trunk twisted,
textured
by thousands
of years of wind.
Clad in a shawl
of bottlebrush
needles and
spiked cones,
your tortured
branches
reach out
like an ancient
arthritic woman
who tries
in vain
to rise
from her chair
and implores me
for a hand up.

Falling

There are days when the gravity
is turned up too high,
when stairs you climb
and descend every day
conspire to bring you down.
Knowing you're in a rush,
they realign themselves
so that your foot fails to find
the familiar support.
Or, as you descend,
they drop,
a subversive escalator,
so that you step out
into air.
In that moment
you know there is
nothing solid beneath you,
that you will soon make landfall,
your reentry inelegant
and painful, and you wish
you could replay that misstep
with more attentiveness and skill.
For that instant you are flying,
but you waste it regretting.
What if you could appreciate
the exhilaration
of being untethered,
the thrill of treading air?
You're going to pay for it anyway.

Wordfall

My words are falling,
bits of a poem
so lyrical they took
flight right
from the keyboard.
But the poem
fizzled, and
I abandoned it,
leaving my words
stranded up there.
Now they tumble
back to earth,
scowling, hurling
epithets at me
as they plop
onto the ground.
Like goose down
escaped from
a comforter
that the dog
has chewed,
the words scatter
everywhere,
making themselves
difficult to retrieve.
I find some clinging
to branches, others
wedged in dense
bushes or stuck
in downspouts.
(I should have used
a larger font.)
Some words splatter
onto the highway
and run in circles,
screaming,
causing accidents.

The authorities are called.
My fallen words
will have something
to say to me,
and it will not
be poetic.
They must be
dusted off,
placated with small
gifts, tasty treats,
persuaded to return
to the poem.
I will promise
never to let them
down again.
And I will fail.

First Warbler of Spring

Along the creek
a minuscule star alights
in the cottonwoods,
and a sweet sweet
flute of song
takes wing.
I raise my binoculars.
There, on a low branch,
filling the frame,
a yellow warbler
tiny and roundish
and oh so yellow—
dandelion yellow,
Crayola yellow–
as though all of
the world's yellow
were concentrated
in this one
small being.

Small Deaths

On a summer morning
laced with the scent
of sage I walk the grassy
meadows and scrub oak
of the ranchland,
making my weekly
check of bluebird nests.

I find four baby birds
dead in their nest,
bodies fused.
Only one more week
and they would have
fledged, flown
free of the nest,
grown feathers
of an azure so intense
it could have been
torn from the sky.

If I were a scientist
I would record their loss,
submit my data,
and be done.
But these small deaths
fly out of my field notes
slip past my armor,
and set loose specters

of those other lives
that might have been.

Bird at Work

A downy
woodpecker,
six inches
of determination,
red nape lit
like a taillight,
hangs upside
down from
a maple branch,
jackhammering
dead wood,
mining a vein
of insects,
his attention so
fixed on his work
he is unaware of me
beneath him,
looking up,
enthralled.

Magpies on Guard

Windy October morning—
persistent rattle
of dried cottonwood leaves
clinging to branches.
Summer's birds gone.
Raucous calls of fussing
magpies, self-appointed
sentries. Caricatures
of security guards
in outlandish uniforms,
they sport caps
with outsized bills, strut
their authority,
dragging their swords
behind them.

Waiting for the Roadrunner

He's a court jester of a bird,
wandering minstrel,
stand-up comic, traveller
from a sillier dimension,

a bird assembled from spare parts—
how else explain that wild crest
or the maniacal look in his eyes,
the absurd feet, the extravagant tail?

Consider his antics. Cartoonlike,
he rushes in, stops short, peers
around corners, cocks his head,
then dashes off to his next gig.

Bird imitating art.

Some days you can catch him
as he sits motionless in the sun,
back feathers spread, absorbing
the sun's energy like a solar panel.

Recharged, he will vanish
into the brush, disappear
so completely you will doubt
you ever saw him.

They tell me the roadrunner
visits this cactus garden every afternoon.
I wait, feeling foolish to be keeping
an appointment with such a bird.

The roadrunner does not come.

Crow Quandary

Some would call it a murder.
I prefer a Hitchcock of crows,

and it has gathered around my garbage can
this frigid morning, the overstuffed container

luring the birds to enjoy its marinated delights.
Still more crows arrive: they inspect, confer in clicks and rattles,

perch on the lid in twos and threes,
but the angled lid is icy, and there's little purchase.

They try to wedge the thing open,
but slide off, flap to the ground cawing.

Still others hop up and try; the group on the ground
urges them on with raucous cries.

They're working together to solve the problem,
and I want them to succeed.

I'm so invested in their process I forget about
the prospect of garbage strewn over the yard.

I remember the movie. Who knows what a Hitchcock might do?
I want to suggest—

*Why don't two or three of you grab onto the lip of the lid
with your feet and then, together, flap your wings?*

But, before they can seize on the solution, the garbage truck arrives,
all menace and roar, and the crows decamp,

the secrets of my household garbage secure for another week.

Crane Fugue

Midwinter
in Bosque del Apache.
Skeletal trees,
grasses faded
to honeyed brown.
Thin crusts of ice
lace the ponds.
In this place
at the end of the day,
the sky gives up
its burden of cranes,
entrusting them
to the water
for the night.

Just at sunset
you can hear them
calling in their
ancient melodies,
necklaces of birds
flying in
to roost,
sky poetry
approaching.
Then the lines
begin to bow,
breaking up into
individual
parachutes
which
descend
to shoreline.

Sandhill cranes,
thousands of them,
balanced on stilts,
fold their wings,

extend extravagant
necks, reaching back
with ebony beaks
to arrange
the silvery bustles
of their tail feathers;
calling to each other
in clarinet trills,
they gather
their young
and wade into
shallow water
to sleep,
tucking their heads
into the soft pillows
of their backs.

At nightfall
two coyotes pace
the shore,
their prey
just out of reach.

The Right Word

I think the air is seeded
with the billions of words
that our E-books jettison
after we finish reading them.
Sprung free, the random words
will float or fly, some bounding,
others tumbling to the ground.
I seldom go out without my word-catcher.
You never know where you'll find
just the right word.

West of Ramona

A row
of rural mailboxes
along the dirt road,
hodgepodge
of receptacles
tilted
at wacky angles,
unsteady
on their posts,
a gaggle
of crimsons,
jades,
cobalt blues,
mustard yellows
crane their necks,
mouths agape
like nestlings
anxious
to be fed.

Sunday Afternoon

After the monotony
of the highway
the park bursts into view,
a constellation
of color and motion;
volleyball nets
stitch webs across
the green expanse,
heads of players pop up
as they leap for the ball.
The outer loop of the park
is a great wheel turning:
runners lope along
interspersed with walkers
and dogs, magnificent dogs:
Greyhounds, Afghans,
Border Collies, Great Danes;
bicycles in all configurations:
racing bikes, tricycles, surreys,
tandems, unicycles;
frisbees cut through
the air to be snatched
and retrieved by
ecstatic retrievers;
nearby, two young men
in tuxedos and yarmulkes
set up a chupa
for a Jewish wedding,
a small family
of rented folding chairs
awaiting the bottoms
of the guests;
young families
with picnic baskets
spread blankets
on the grass;
snowy egrets fly in,

land among fishermen
on the lake shore,
and side by side, they
fish for their supper.

II. Off the Map

Migrations

Birding along the border in the shadow of Tijuana,
eyes alert for the rufous-crowned sparrow,
I begin to read another story inscribed in the trail.
A blue shirt, part of a shoe, flattened water bottles,
a bicycle frame without wheels
abandoned in the dash for cover,
dropped while dodging the searchlights.

Unbidden, an image surfaces of another time
and other border crossings made at night and on foot.
My father, a little boy, riding atop the bundles
in a wooden cart pushed by his brothers
over broken roads, his mother and sisters
plodding behind, their shoes wearing thin.
Cold clawing through coats and blankets.
Fleeing pogroms. Walking across Poland
all the way to the sea.

What's Left Behind

A green-winged teal
lands on the pond,
his cinnamon head and
iridescent green whoosh
unmistakable.
He dabbles in the muck,
seeming not to mind
the sludge in his soup,
a marinating stew of garbage
that forms a foamy scum
on the water's surface.

Here at the foot of the country,
down the ravine from the border
where spring rains leave lagoons,
the slimy water is clogged
with trash and belongings
jettisoned by migrants on the run.

The detritus of the desperate:
orange peels, half-eaten burritos,
baby food jars, empty liter bottles,
styrofoam coolers, a soccer ball.
Not to mention the discarded shorts,
socks, and tee shirts,
as though a backyard clothesline
had been swamped
by floodwaters and carried here.

The undocumented,
the frightened
cross at night,
shed all but the essentials.
Worn out shoes fall apart
while you're running for cover.
Better to go barefoot into your new life.

Footholds

The sand dunes rise from the valley floor
in the photograph, mountains
made of wind-lashed sand
torn over time from other mountains.

In the distance two tiny figures climb
the S-curved ridge. Footprints of disturbed
sediment tumble down with each step,
and I sink in the loose strata.

My dog frolics by my side, so lightweight
he seems to float above the surface.
The top of the dune comes into view,
but when we reach the crest there will be another

higher dune and still another and another after that.
No matter. In the picture we are young,
there is plenty of time. One step forward,
half step back, we climb.

Hernandez, 1991

After *Moonrise, Hernandez, New Mexico,*
Ansel Adams, 1941

I remember this place,
though I've never been here before.
We stand at the edge of the road,
the pueblo still recognizable.

The adobe church has a new tin roof,
and the wooden crosses
have multiplied in the graveyard,
consecrated with plastic flowers.

The trees have grown taller, but the peaks
of the Sangre de Cristos are unchanged,
and the village endures, isolated
in the mesquite scrub of the valley.

Two young boys scramble
up the embankment. Dark eyes study us.
The older boy asks–
Señora, why do people always stop here?

I open the book, show them *Moonrise.*
His finger traces the image of the pueblo,
stops on a squat adobe building.
–*That's my house!*

A Sidelong Look

After *George Bernard Shaw*
Photograph by Yousuf Karsh, 1943

George Bernard Shaw has just made a joke
at the expense of the photographer,
a subtle jest by the great wit of the century,

and he turns in his chair, cocks his head to see
if the man with the camera appreciates his rarified humor.
He savors his *bon mot* as Karsh nails the shot.

The playwright is possessed of a psyche
too boundless to capture on film.
His eyes flash as he readies his next repartee.

Shaw tugs the chain of his lorgnette; long arthritic
fingers clutch the spectacles; both his bushy white eyebrows
and bristling beard emit electrical signals.

Is it his outsized ego that compels him to sit
for his portrait with the great Karsh,
photographer of the world's luminaries?

Or, maybe he believes Karsh to be a Pygmalion
who will render an image of him so animate
it will speak in his voice long after he's gone.

The photo hangs on the wall above the couch.
Matted and framed, Shaw ponders humanity's foolishness.
His eyes penetrate the glass; he is about to speak.

November Nests

High in a cottonwood a hawk's aerie
braces on sturdy branches.

A woven oriole's nest dangles from the tip
of a bough like a forgotten sock.

Nestled into the V of two crabapple limbs,
a robin's cup of grass and mud.

Skeletal trees expose last summer's nests,
ruins silhouetted against slate sky.

I see them only now, their job done:
eggs hatched, young nurtured, fledged.

Used husks remain.

~

Last spring's magpie nest,
still visible in the blue spruce.

For days the female paced
back and forth

beside her nest tree,
shrieking her grief and rage,

her nest invaded, eggs devoured
by marauding squirrels.

Her mate stood by,
powerless to soothe her.

I heard her cries
and knew.

~

I remember the failed nest
and the empty womb,

the proto-lives that vanished
before they ever were,

the promise unkept,
the body's betrayal,

a blip on the ultrasound,
then gone.

A History of You

for Daniel

There was a time
when you
remembered
how to fly,
a time before
you took
human shape–
when your
plumage
was bright
and fresh
and you carried
the secret
knowledge
of one
who has touched
the sky.

There was a time
when you sang
in your ancient
language
from a perch high
in the primeval
canopy,
where you fed
on sweet nectar,
like a god.

There was a time
when you
came down
from the trees
to wander
on foot,
carrying all
your lives

in a silken sack
slung over
your shoulder.

You wandered,
who knows
how long,
until the day
that gate,
the one
that had always
been closed
to us,
swung open,
and we entered
trembling,
saw you
for the first time,
held you,
and brought you
home.

Catching the School Bus

One by one they shoot out of the house,
projectiles launched at one minute intervals,
four tow-headed boys in stairstep sizes,
brothers burning the half block race to the bus stop.
You can feel the bass rumble
before the bus appears,
hear its asthmatic wheeze
as it struggles up the hill, anticipate
the metallic complaint of its brakes,
its voiceprint unchanged
in the twenty years since
you were the boy running for that bus.
Each boy leans into the effort,
his forward momentum so strong
that all that keeps these wispy creatures
from taking flight is the ballast of
their overstuffed, oversized backpacks,
as if the backpacks have sprouted legs,
carrying their boy cargo forward
to carefully deposit it
into the cradle of the school bus.

On the Day That You Left

The horizon tilted
and the color drained
out of the world.

I've heard that
in Russia under the tsars
Jewish boys were
sometimes kidnapped
from their shtetls and
forced into the army–
to serve for twenty-five years.
Few ever returned.

It must be in my DNA
this horror of armies,
this terror for my son,
and it detonated like
an improvised explosive device
when you enlisted
and burned like
a refinery fire
until the day
you came home.

Uncommon Ground

A golden eagle soars on a thermal,
and we stop to track its flight.

Women of a certain age,
our necks bent under the weight

of binoculars and cameras,
we sport floppy sun hats

and sensible shoes, our pockets lumpy
with water bottles and field guides.

We listen for bird sounds but hear instead
the rhythmic thud of boots on the trail.

Seven men move single file,
uniformed in camouflage,

solemn as soldiers
before battle, hunting rifles slung

over shoulders, faces smeared
with black war paint.

A darker, more sinister forest
passes through this one.

On the First Day of the New Administration

We wake to find
the bed sliding
across the floor,
the horizon skewed.
Those now in charge
have caused our planet
to wobble free of its axis.
We are informed that
the laws of gravity
have been suspended.
Earth has moved out
of its old neighborhood,
slipped its orbit
shifted its weight
and is screeching
through space.

We rock and lurch.
Some lose their footing,
tumble off the planet.
The rest scramble to grasp
something solid,
while bridges
and buildings buckle
and fall, trees topple,
tigers wander free
from the zoo, waves
slosh ashore
from once-placid lakes,
dormant volcanoes erupt,
the oceans rise
and the sky goes black.

And this is only the first day.

In the Night

All morning
boisterous flocks
of crows converge
on my neighbor's
yard. Is that
a red tarp
on the ground?
No, not a tarp,
but the bloody
carcass of a deer,
torn open,
partially eaten.

Those bone-
chilling howls
in the night–
coyotes
celebrating
the kill.
It must have
taken a
whole pack
to bring down
a deer.

I tell myself
not to get upset–
it's only coyotes
hunting
in the night,
not insurgents, or
invading armies
or secret police;
only wild animals
being eaten.

There's nothing
we can do.

On a Ragged Point

I stand alone
on a ragged point
high above
a rocky shore.
Fogged in,
tucked in,
bony fingers
of cypress
cling to the edge.
Droplets make
the air palpable,
spider webs purled
by tendrils of mist,
dancing veils
of light and fog,
no hard edges,
no visible decay,
liquid silver
flowing.
Far below
the onslaught
of the tides,
relentless
bass of water
assaulting rock.
Otherworldly shapes
of cliffs emerge.
Tied neither
to earth
nor sea,
naked rock
floats free.
Above it all
the spiral aria
of the canyon wren.

Harlequin

Up and down the rocky coast
I searched for you
in tumultuous waves
that pummel the cliffs.

In the silvery mist
I scanned the surf
again and again,
and waited.

Flotillas of dark birds swam by–
surf scoters with
outsized orange bills,
pigeon guillemots
kicking vermillion feet.

But you were not among them,
commedia dell'arte trickster,
harlequin duck,
histrionicus histrionicus.

You left me hanging
over the edge of a cliff,
desperate for a glimpse
of a duck.

Family Shooting

It's right there in the state park–
the sign along the road heralds
the *Family Shooting Center*,
like a place you could bring the whole family–
ma, pa, granny, gramps, Billy and Susie—
and shoot them all.

It's hard to get used to the rattle
of gunfire as you walk the park trails,
looking and listening for birds.
You glimpse a tiny yellow warbler,
hear its delicate song, and
BOOM! the deep bass of gunfire
reverberates, and your brain
screams *Hit the ground!*

You know better, of course—
it's just those families
shooting one another–
but still… you've got to wonder
what the birds must be thinking.

Misbehaving Metaphors

My metaphors are misbehaving again,
growling and hissing, some even snarling
at one another. They must be separated,
placed in time out to simmer down and
contemplate the cause of their bad behavior.
Is it disappointment with the poem itself?
Or resentment at being relegated to
less prominent positions? Perhaps they are
jealous of younger, lovelier images.
Do they think I've made them sound
dry and stale? Or that I've
let them fall flat on their faces?
Or neglected them in favor of fresher,
more muscular metaphors?
They mutter and sulk. I worry,
will they leave me for another poet?
I tell them we simply can't have
this bickering inside the poem—
it will undermine its foundation,
cause its walls to sag, its floors to buckle,
its doors to stick. But metaphorical
feelings have been hurt, egos bruised.
It will take time for them to heal.
They're damned prima donnas,
those metaphors.

What Emily Might Have Said
About Poetic Voice

With apologies to Emily Dickinson

Voice is the thing with beak and claws—
That perches in your head—
And writes the poem with all its flaws—
About the thing you dread—

But who of us has time to waste—
To search for phantom "Voice"?
It's high time the truth was faced—
We really have no choice—

Voice is who we are—My friends—
It's part of our Genome—
Not some mask we might append—
It's our voice that makes the poem.

Stacking the Bookpile

Late afternoon,
daylight dwindles,
snow falls.
I lay in a cord
of books
to ward off
the bleakness
of the months
to come.
They say
ancient peoples
watched
with dread
as the days
grew darker.
All winter
I will light
my way with
the flame
of a book,
the words
crackling.

A Road Map of My Brain at Sixty-Six

Studying the map of my brain,
trying to find my way
to wherever it is I'm going,
I come upon strange
twisted, gnarled paths,
roads that lead to ruins,
dead ends.

Some of those thoroughfares
are impassible, overgrown
with knotted foliage,
leading to once thriving,
now decayed civilizations.
At the end of one
such road lies
the fossilized remains
of my law practice.

A pockmarked trail
leads to a pile of
crumbled rocks
under which lies, lifeless,
any inclination I ever had
to serve on a committee.

A weed-choked path
wends into strangling
bramble, under which
I find, crushed and still,
what was once my desire
to grow a garden.

A dark and nameless
potholed side street,
perpetually under construction,
leads to what remains of
my urge to cook.

But, look, over here
there's a tree-lined
sunlit trail where I
go to watch birds.
I can feel their poetry
like fireworks lighting up
every single synapse.
I want to walk that path
every day, explore its twists
and turns, its curves
and switchbacks,
as it propels me
right off the map.

III. A Brief Passage

Murmuration

From a distance
you might mistake it
for a cloud of smoke
as it spreads across
the canvas
of prairie sky,
shape-shifting,
roiling, tumultuous,
first a dancing
funnel cloud,
then an elephant
rolling over,
a dragon rearing up,
a galaxy spinning,
then collapsing,
a phantasmagoria
formed by a myriad
of starlings locked
in labyrinthine ballet,
each image lasting
only an instant,
then dissolving,
as if a passage
to another universe
had revealed itself
and then vanished.

Hailstorm

On a September
afternoon the sky
churns up a storm cloud
the color of charcoal,
which descends
in a dousing of rain,
then a fusillade
of hailstones.
What was up
has come down—
tree branches,
shredded leaves,
roof shingles,
nails, crabapples,
frisbees,
tennis balls
strewn over
the yard.
Naked trees,
bludgeoned roofs,
battered cars,
shattered windows,
as if we needed
another lesson
in impermanence.
The house finch,
his song cut short,
washed away
from his roof perch
into the rain gutter,
down the downspout,
drowned.

Flocked

I am being watched
by a flock of birds.
From above
I hear the high
tinkling bell sound
of bushtits, tiny grey
birds who zoom in
inches from my face,
then stuff themselves
into the suet feeder
by the dozens,
oblivious to my
outsized presence.
I can feel the small
wind of their wings.
Red-breasted nuthatches
swoop down, one, then
two, tooting like toy
trumpets, then an array
of chickadees chattering
to each other as they
snag their food—*over
here! It's better on
this side!*—they snatch
seeds and bounce off
to cache them in
the ponderosas.
A downy woodpecker
joins the foragers,
his red nape aflame
in the sunlight, close
enough for me to touch.
For a few perfect minutes
I am *in* this frenzied flock
of feeding birds.
I could be one of them,
as if this were an edge,

a threshold into a
dimension devoted
to the comings and
goings of birds,
invisible to most,
only *I* am granted
this brief passage
into their sphere.

That House on Berry Avenue

A young family has bought
the house behind mine,
the shroud of tangled foliage
that obscured the dwelling
hacked down and cleared away,
the drapes, always closed, now gone,
the naked structure revealed
in the throes of renovation.

I can see all the way through
the ground floor,
its windows squinting in the
unfamiliar light,
its walls ripped down
to skeletal studs.

I wonder if they know
that this house was infested
with misfortune:
the years she never left the house,
the walls absorbing
the toxins of her melancholy,
the decades of caring
for her paralyzed son,
the loss of a daughter,
and then the son.

Sorrow has permeated
the floor boards,
seeped into the foundation–
a residue of heartache
has settled into the ground
and mixed with the soil,
harmless until
something stirs it up.

Cancer Pavilion

I enter the building
marked "Cancer Pavilion"
in ten-foot high letters,
as if to confront
the disease,
stare it down,
manage the fear.
In the lobby I pass
spectral patients
in treatment,
the unnaturally thin,
the hairless. I want
to explain myself:
Excuse me,
I'll just be a minute.
I really don't belong here.
I'm cured, you see;
just here for a follow-up,
not for surgery
or radiation or chemo,
like you.
I feel myself stepping
too heavily through
the lobby,
taking up too much
space in the elevator,
my conspicuous health
giving offense
to the others
in the oncologist's
waiting room.
I am not one of them:
my color is too good,
my hair too firmly attached,
my posture too straight,

while they endure
the interminable waiting
sunken in their chairs,
eyes fixed on something
I cannot see.

Looking Up

Windy spring afternoon,
lake empty of birds,
iridescent flashes
of light high above,
like a miniature galaxy
visible in daytime,
so high I can barely
make sense of the shape.
I squint into the brightness,
try to organize this image
in my brain. Yes,
I know this pattern.
A troupe of white pelicans
dances on thermals,
wheels and spirals,
soars in flocks
that merge and split,
and merge and split again,
like a cell dividing,
as sunlight reflects
off their luminescent wings.
Disdaining the grey,
choppy waters of the lake,
they've flown aloft
to swim in air, frolic
on wind currents,
while I cling to the earth
in wonder.

Unraveling

Vagueness falls over you like a veil.
The warp and weft of your tapestry slackens,
multihued threads loosen, fray.

Your stories meander, search
for a way through the weave,
snag in tangled strands.

You pick up another yarn,
follow it as far as the next snarl,
put it down, begin again.

We've been friends so long
our stories intertwine,
your fabric is part of mine.

Is this the way it happens?
Not with a dimming of lights
or a slow erasure?

I see in your canvas
what I dread in my own,
a dwindling

barely detectable,
until it ties your mind
into knots.

Intermission

for Henry

An eerie purplish light hovers
over the ancients in the concert audience
after the Beethoven string quartet.

We look about, alarmed, pinch the skin
on the backs of our hands,
check the mirror for our reflections,
locate our car keys,
touch one another.

The faces of the old
turn translucent, their hair
spiderweb thin. As they dodder
into the lobby, something unseen
liberates them from their wobbly legs,
crooked spines, traitorous joints.

They gather in earnest ghostly groups,
ask each other,
Was it something in the music?
and ponder the advantages:
no more pain, no medicines or special diets.
Some make plans to downsize again,
or even travel, now that there's time.

Discarded canes, walkers, wheelchairs,
oxygen tanks litter the room.
You can hear the spirits squeal
as they levitate through the lobby,
luminescent and giddy,
flinging their hearing aids into the air.

Snowy Egret

Swathed
in veils of
white plumes,
she steps
high through
shallows
on ebony
stilts,
heedless
of her
reflection.
Immersed
in fishing,
she focuses
hard on the
bottom,
her feet
probing
the mud
for prey.
Her wiggling
golden toes
must look
like fish
to the fish,
who never
see the
swift strike
of her
rapier
beak.

Leafbirds

Leaves tumble
from already bare
maple branches.
As they touch the
ground, they
become birds–
red, and do I see
yellow ones?
Finches?
But packed
so tightly together
on a snowbank,
foraging with
such intensity that
I grab binoculars
to be sure.

Not house finches,
but red crossbills!
A nomadic flock
seeking pinecone seeds,
the males dull red,
the females yellow,
mountain birds
so rare in town,
landing for
a drink of snow
and a snack
outside my
front window,
materializing
like a poem.

Three Moons

Moonrise silvers
the snowy Sangre de Cristos
as the last streaks of sunlight
turn fiery gold
the rough-hewn crosses
in the little graveyard
behind the pueblo church.

~

Blood Moon in eclipse,
so eerily crimson,
swollen, alien,
it could be
some celestial object
newly captured
by our planet's gravity,
not shining on its own,
but borrowing
its terracotta hue
from the Earth.

~

The full moon crouches
on the horizon,
yellow and inflated
as a second sun,
then pulls itself up
over the marsh
as seven sandhill cranes
cross in silhouette.

Owl Duet

For Mark

Call and response fly back and forth
on silent wings.

Will you come?
Yes, I will.

A great horned owl hoots
high in the blue spruce outside our window.

His deep bass resonates
against the mantle of darkness and snowfall.

Quiet, then an answering *hoo hoo*
from a distance.

Two owls duetting.
I imagine them an old mated pair

like us, only reunited mid-winter,
rekindling their bond,

while we, well past the anxieties
of nesting and raising young,

spend the evening
in our own call and response,

me writing this poem
for you.

Adrift

White fluff aloft,
a down feather
floats free
on a breath of air.
Fugitive from
a bird's breast,
it drifts
in zigs and zags
on its final flight.
No longer bird,
no longer of any use,
its filaments wiggle,
collapse into
ever smaller
silken threads
that vanish
into the grass.
One day you may
find me adrift
in just such
slow descent,
disintegrating.

Uninhabited Planet

Diminutive,
asteroidlike,
the rock rotates
on its wobbly axis,
spurting
maroon volcanoes.
Silvery liquids
cascade down
its slopes,
nourish what might be
mosses and lichens
blooming below.
A daisy-shaped
moon, or maybe
it's a spaceship,
pirouettes
around its host,
leaving a trail
of what look like
bubbles.
A great cobalt spot
sprouts on one flank:
smaller blue blotches
surface and coalesce,
but only if
you stare at it
for a long time.
Undiscovered,
unpopulated,
safe from collision
with comets, planets
or space debris,
encased
in its glass globe,
it sits on my desk
in perfect peace.

Dancing with Cranes

In spring in Monte Vista
the sandhill cranes dance.
One bird begins, and the urge
to dance sweeps through the flock,
as though the earth
were rippling under their feet.

The long-legged birds bow
and leap, wings flapping
as if to shake off
the weight of winter,
then launch into jetés,
glides, pirouettes.

Mated pairs dance together,
hopeful males swagger
before the single ladies,
tentative youngsters watch,
then one by one, toe out
to make their own dance.

From the road, a gaggle of birders
observes through binoculars
and spotting scopes;
photographers with
artillery-sized lenses
capture the spectacle in pixels.

Only the poet sees that a passage
has opened to another world.
She climbs through the portal
onto the sandbar
into the flock
and joins the dance.

Lois Levinson is a graduate of the Poetry Book Project at Lighthouse Writers Workshop in Denver, Colorado. She is the author of the chapbook, *Crane Dance*, published by Finishing Line Press. Her poems have appeared in *Bird's Thumb, Clementine Poetry Journal, The Corner Club Press, These Fragile Lilacs, Mountain Gazette, The Literary Nest, Gravel, Literary Mama, Yew Journal* and *Mount Hope.*

CPSIA information can be obtained
at www.ICGtesting.com
Printed in the USA
FFOW02n2357220318
45819523-46709FF